More OFFBEAT BRISTOL

JAMES BELSEY

REDCLIFFE
Bristol

First published in 1993 by
Redcliffe Press Ltd
49 Park St, Bristol.

© James Belsey

ISBN 1 872971 92 X

British Library Cataloguing-in-Publication Data.
A catalogue record for this book is available
from the British Library.

Typeset and printed by
The Longdunn Press Ltd, Bristol

Contents

Bristol's sea-going church

St Michael's Hill is one of the prettiest streets in Bristol with its picturesque setting and collection of fine old buildings.

And none of the buildings are prettier than the delightful almshouses which Bristol merchant Edward Colston built for the poor and needy after buying a three acre site on St Michael's Hill for £100 in 1691.

Colston spent a further £2,500 having the attractive almshouses built around an elegant courtyard with, as the centrepiece, a delightful little barrel-vaulted chapel. Its most unusual feature? The panelled walls . . . made of old ships' timbers.

The chapel played a central role in the lives of the 24 residents, for Colston insisted that the only people housed must be Bristol-born and regular Church of England church-goers.

Colston had made an immense fortune, much of it from the slave trade, and the almshouses were the first of many gifts made to Bristol. It's possible some of these timbers are from his slaving ships which used to sail the lucrative triangular passage from Bristol to Africa to the American colonies and back.

The day Bob Hope came home to Bristol

When Bob Hope, Hollywood's wisecracking top comedian, came to find his roots in Bristol, he caused a near-riot.

It happened on Saturday August 30th, 1952 when Bob told his chauffeur to drive his limousine to 326 Whitehall Road, his home in toddler days.

Bob had played two sell-out shows at the Colston Hall the night before. Between appearances the *Evening Post* took one of his former Whitehall neighbours backstage to meet the star in his dressing room.

She told him how she remembered the four-year-old boy who had emigrated to the United States with his family in 1907 and gone on to find fame and fortune in smash hits like the Road comedies with Bing Crosby.

Bob noted the address of his one-time Bristol home and, as he set off for the next leg of the tour, decided to take a look. When his big car drew up outside the house so he could inspect the place and take some shots with his movie camera, a large, noisy crowd quickly gathered to gaze at the Hollywood star and exchange jokes.

'I have carried with me ever since a permanent and forcible reminder of Bristol. This is it,' he said, tapping a scar on his right temple.

'Brother, how well I remember it. I had a little dog as a pet and one day I saw boys ill-treating it near the house. I ran out and to try to protect it and one of them threw a stone. It got me on the temple.'

But there were no ill-feelings, he added . . . just some scar tissue to mark his days as a Bristol boy.

Bristol's own Bob Hope . . . he caused a near riot when he returned to his childhood home in Whitehall Road.

The tree that changed Bristol

It was planted in October 1973 outside the ancient Hatchet Inn in Frogmore Street, a Norway maple or Acer Platanoides if you want to use its correct botanical name.

And it marks the start of a revolution that has transformed many parts of Bristol from tree-less, green-less areas to ones with hardly a corner which doesn't have a flourishing display of boughs, branches and leaves.

That historic planting was by the Bristol Civic Society as part of its 'Plant A Tree For 73' campaign. The small band of enthusiasts who attended the ceremony couldn't have known what they had started.

The 1973 tree-planting campaign was such a success that they decided to continue it the following year . . . and the year after . . . and the year after that.

In fact it's been going ever since and thousands of trees have been planted – all thanks to that one Norway maple and the stir it created.

Mr Mcadam's testing mouthful

John Loudon Mcadam's idea was very simple . . . that the best roads were made from smaller stones.

His method, he was convinced, would be cheap, effective and could transform Bristol's roads from boulder-strewn quagmires in wet weather and rutted obstacles in the dry to good, solid, smooth surfaces.

Mr Mcadam was appointed Bristol's roads surveyor in 1815 and put his plan into action. It worked. In fact it worked so successfully that his roads provided 'an example that has been followed and imitated from one end of the kingdom to the other'.

But – a very important but – how to ensure that the stones were small enough for a Mcadam road? Stone-breaking gangs would be only too happy to get away with larger lumps of rock and so save themselves the trouble of yet more work to break them down to the surveyor's 6 oz maximum limit.

So Mr Mcadam invented just the test to keep his gangs on their mettle. If a stone looked too big, he insisted it was promptly popped into the breaker's mouth. And if it wouldn't fit in the mouth, it had to be broken again. The lesson was soon learned . . . and the stones stayed small.

The Norway maple tree that began the greening of Bristol in a huge tree planting operation.

9

Cavaliers and Roundheads . . . and Bristol's weak spot

The plaque calls it Washington's Breach, but it's hard to imagine what could be breached on busy Queen's Road in Clifton.

In fact when the Civil War broke out between King Charles I and Parliament, this spot stood along the defences thrown up by the city fathers to try to protect Bristol.

Parliamentary supporters found refuge in Bristol early in the war and King Charles ordered the city to be taken by his nephew Prince Rupert.

Finding a weak spot in the defences was the trick and one of the Prince's commanders, Colonel Washington – ancestor of George Washington, founding President of the United States – pulled it off. He and his forces ran forward from near today's Victoria Rooms, found shelter from gunfire from nearby forts and then made their attack on the defences, hurling hand grenades and routing the defenders.

They were soon down to College Green and it wasn't long before Bristol surrendered to two years of Royalist rule.

FROM NEAR THIS PLACE
ON JULY 26TH 1643
COLONEL HENRY WASHINGTON
ATTACKED THE PARLIAMENTARY DEFENCES
BETWEEN ROYAL FORT AND BRANDON HILL

WITH A SMALL FORCE HE EFFECTED
"WASHINGTONS BREACH"
(AT THE PRESENT JUNCTION OF PARK ROW AND PARK STREET)
THROUGH WHICH THE ROYALIST TROOPS ENTERED
BRISTOL AND COMPELLED ITS CAPITULATION

HE WAS THE GRANDSON OF LAWRENCE WASHINGTON
OF SULGRAVE AND A COLLATERAL ANCESTOR OF
GEORGE WASHINGTON (1732-1799)
FIRST PRESIDENT OF
THE UNITED STATES OF AMERICA

When the balloon first went up . . . and landed in St George

It's altogether fitting that the first hot air balloon to be seen in Britain soared over Bristol's skies and landed in St George.

With modern Bristol the hot air ballooning capital of the world thanks to the efforts of Don Cameron, how right that when pioneer balloon-maker Mr Dinwiddie's unmanned hot air balloon came to rest after its historic flight from Bath, it landed in what has become Bristol.

The event caused such a sensation that local folk named the landing site Air Balloon Hill, and the name has stuck ever since, with the local pub named after the event.

In France in 1783 the Montgolfiers burned straw and wool beneath silk bags to invent lighter-than-air flight and the news of their balloons caused a sensation.

Mr Dinwiddie and a friend Dr Parry were hard on their heels with a double launch on Saturday January 10th, 1784. Dr Parry's vanished without trace but Mr Dinwiddie's flew west along the Avon valley to its place in British aviation history.

John Cleese's silly walk

From the moment gangly comic John Cleese gave his knee-twisting, leg-sailing performance in the Ministry of Silly Walks sketch on the classic *Monty Python's Flying Circus* show (left), the world was hooked.

And when he gave a repeat in that infamous episode of 'Fawlty Towers' when he broke into a crazed goosestep before a party of German visitors, we knew we were seeing one of the greatest comedy routines of them all.

The first performance of the Cleese silly walk? When the comedian was a schoolboy at Clifton College in the 1950s.

Already gawky but an avid cricket player, Cleese used his awkward gait to invent silly walks to annoy the cricket coach and to win popularity. He wasn't, he admitted, a popular boy and thought he could make friends by being funny.

There is even a school report from that time which refers to the 'many Cleesian glides' on the cricket field, a sure reference to the leggy gait he was developing into his show-stopping gag.

But while he may have been a prankster on the cricket field, he was also a good player. He even bowled out top English cricketer Denis Compton in a game between Clifton and the MCC.

The mystery of Crew's Hole

Crew's Hole . . . it's one of the oddest names of any suburb in Bristol and it has one of the most colourful legends, of smugglers, contraband and midnight sorties.

Crew's Hole is a little riverside place on the northern bank of the Avon opposite St Anne's and in the old days, before Bristol's Floating Harbour was built in the early nineteenth century, the river was tidal.

That meant easy access from the busy City Docks with its bustling international trade and its valuable cargoes.

So the name Crew's Hole? Local legend insists that it was just that . . . a sanctuary or hiding place where the crews of the ocean going vessels hid contraband.

It was certainly a good spot to store valuables. The Avon had a thriving riverborne trade between Bristol, Bath and Bradford-on-Avon and Crew's Hole was a perfect place from which to send crews up-river with wine, brandy and other goodies which had escaped the attention of the Revenue Men.

Peaceful now . . . but was Crew's Hole by the Avon the place where returning crews hid their gold and contraband?

It must be added that the name Crew's is also believed to be a corruption of Scruze, perhaps a local landowner and that hole could all too well refer to one of the local coalmines.

But most of us prefer the legend of Crew's Hole, the Smugglers' Refuge.

Overdressed in Bristol fashion

Henry Tudor found Bristol girls shipshape and Bristol fashion . . . in fact rather too fashionable for a city claiming it was down on its luck.

Henry, who had recently defeated Richard III at Bosworth Field and been crowned as Henry VII, founder of the Tudor dynasty, first came to Bristol as King in 1486.

Henry, a notoriously money-minded man, was on his travels in an effort to squeeze as much cash as he could from his subjects. Bristol was well prepared for his visit.

The city's merchants told him tale after tale of Bristol's appalling financial state. The citizens were in no position to hand out more than a pittance to the Royal coffers, they wailed.

The disappointed monarch was suspicious. On his return a few years later those same merchants and their families entertained his Majesty as royally as they could – too royally for the King to be fooled any longer into believing that Bristol was broke.

The food was excellent, the wines wonderful and he noted with delight the good looks, the rich clothes and the sparkling jewels of the Bristol beauties he met.

He announced that Bristol corporation had to stump up £500 to the crown on the spot and that every Bristolian worth £200 or more had to pay a levy of £1.

When the astonished citizens heard his verdict and asked why this sudden sting, the cheerful monarch replied that he had seen that Bristol could well afford the tax hike 'because men's wives went so sumptuously apparelled.'

15

Hang 'em high

I can't think of a drearier corner of Bristol than where the ruins of the New Gaol gate glower over the New Cut on Cumberland Road.

I'm sure the city workers who park their cars in Bedminster and Southville and walk by the gate each day must feel the same momentary depression I feel whenever I see this grim relic.

This granite gatehouse with mock portcullis was designed with a flat roof and a trap door for public hangings. A special scaffold was made for the hangman's visit, and these grisly events never failed to attract huge crowds.

The first to be hanged before the mob was a young lad who, in a fit of passion, had killed his lover. So many people turned up for the show that there were notices warning the crowds of the danger of being shouldered into the New Cut by the press of the mob.

The last to die was an 18-year-old servant girl Sarah Thomas who was driven to kill her mistress after years of ill-treatment and bullying. She screamed, howled, sobbed and pleaded throughout every last ghastly moment of her life and even the prison governor was so overcome that he fainted.

It was Bristol's last public hanging and the horror and revulsion it caused became an unforgettable memory for the citizens who witnessed this pathetic event.

The gaol itself was closed in 1883 and sold to the Great Western Railway. The company used it as a coal yard.

The stark, sinister ruins of New Gaol gate on Cumberland Road . . . it once echoed to the screams of prisoners at public executions.

16

Buried treasure of the blitz

When the bombs started raining down on Bristol the night of the first great blitz, well-known jeweller Mr Chillcott of Chillcott's in Park Street was more worried about his gold, silver and jewels than he was for his own skin.

Park Street was one of the worst-hit areas that night of Sunday November 24th, 1940 but luckily Chillcott's, established in 1808, was left standing in the sea of smoke, flames and rubble.

Standing, but wide open to temptation from looters who could easily have crawled in through the broken windows. Looting blitzed properties was one of the more unsavoury features of 'our finest hour'.

So Mr Chillcott ignored the dangers, collected all the most expensive items he could carry from the shop and escaped through a trap door to the street outside.

As the bombs continued to fall he hurried to the graveyard of St George's Church just up the hill and secretly buried a fortune in valuables.

The next morning, as shattered Bristolians surveyed the wreck of Park Street, Mr Chillcott returned to the graveyard and recovered the 'loot'.

The night the Beatles 'bombed' in Bristol

Tuesday November 10th, 1964 is one of pop music's notable dates, the last night of the final full-length Beatles' British tour . . . and the night John, Paul, George and Ringo were well and truly bombed!

The place was the Colston Hall where the Fab Four headed a ten-act bill which also included top Tamla Motown singer Mary 'My Guy' Wells.

The Beatles were paid £850 for their two Bristol shows and there was an end-of-term euphoria at the close of an astonishing tour and an extraordinary year in which Beatlemania had become a worldwide phenomenon.

The film *A Hard Day's Night* had rocketed them to top of the box office charts at the world's cinemas, they had sold records by the million and their American tour had been one of the greatest successes in showbiz history. And all within little more than ten months.

Towards the end of the second show – with girls screaming so loudly you couldn't hear a note they played or a word they sang – some bright spark who'd clambered into the roof space high above the stage dropped a bag of flour on the world's most famous superstars.

The bag exploded perfectly, covering the Beatles with flour. Ringo had to clear his drums while John, Paul and George fell about, shrieking with laughter.

No one claimed responsibility but the prank was probably the work of one of the road crew, part of the tradition of end-of-tour fun and games.

The Beatles did play a very brief British tour the following year but by then they'd had more than enough of life on the road.

And the number they were playing when the flour tumbled that night in Bristol? 'If I Fell'.

The Beatles in 1964 . . . John could have done with that umbrella when flour bombers struck their Bristol show.

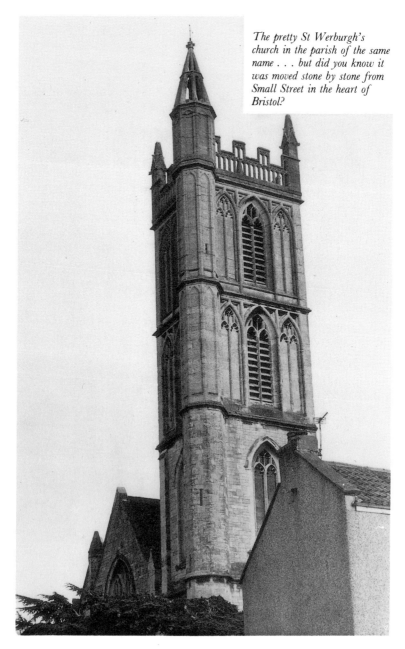

The pretty St Werburgh's church in the parish of the same name . . . but did you know it was moved stone by stone from Small Street in the heart of Bristol?

St Werburgh's . . . a church on the move

Victorian Bristolians thought big and bold, and when a well-loved, centuries-old church began to get in the way of the major re-developments in the city centre, the church had to go.

The building was St Werburgh's in Small Street, a handsome part of old Bristol's history with its fine tower and decorated exterior. Unfortunately it happened to be in the wrong place by the end of the 1870s.

The building had already been saved a century before when it was claimed to be unsafe, but an appeal raised enough money to keep it standing. In 1878, with the east end blocking an increasingly important artery in central Bristol, even an appeal couldn't save St Werburghs.

So it was demolished . . . but very, very carefully. Major bits and pieces were transported a mile or so east and painstakingly fitted together jigsaw-style into a new St Werburgh's in the area that now carries its name.

The other bits of old St Werburgh's had a more ignominious end. They were spirited off to non-ecclesiastical sites across the city where the weathered stone was re-used in new buildings.

Mr Knee's transport knees-up

The great container revolution, it's always said, was one of the wonders of post-war years.

That was when, the story goes, standardised containers which slipped on and off lorries, trains and ships with equal ease arrived and took off in a big way, changing the face of the freight business.

Not true at all. Bristol knew all about container shipping more than a century before today's big boxes began fetching goods to and fro . . . and William Knee is the man who deserves all the credit.

He'd opened a depot in Temple Street, near the new Temple Meads station, when the railways began and, within a few years, he announced a spectacular new service, the Knee's Furniture Van For The Removal Of Furniture etc Without Packing.

21

It was a brilliant invention and an instant success. His wheeled vehicles fitted neatly aboard Great Western flatbed wagons to provide the first roll-on, roll-off service of them all. You loaded your Knee's van outside your own home, it travelled by road and rail and was delivered to the front door of your new house.

Knee's road'n'rail furniture vans did a roaring trade until shortly before World War I . . . providing the very first model for today's global container trade.

Pie Poudre . . . and instant justice

The sign still hangs over the Stag and Hounds pub on Old Market – Pie Poudre Court, Established 1483.

But only keen local historians and those with memories of a quaint annual ceremony know that this was once the spot where instant justice was handed out to pickpockets, cheats and thieves when Old Market really was a market.

Pie Poudre? It's a rough-ish piece of French which means Pie (pied, or foot) and Poudre (powder) and together they form an expression meaning 'dusty feet' or ragamuffins.

Market days always attracted suspicious characters and petty crimes, but detaining suspects for a later trial over trivial offences was a costly nuisance. Hence the Pie Poudre Court to mete out immediate fines, punishments or imprisonment.

At first it met under an oak tree where the Stag and Hounds now stands and then, the legend goes, it moved to an upstairs room inside the pub.

There was an annual ceremony to mark the court's opening in which food and drink were served, but rowdies who had downed too much free ale and cider often spoiled the proceedings, so it was suppressed in 1870.

A scaled-down version – without the booze – continued until 1973 although the court itself had been abandoned a century before.

The Bristolian
who invented the
movies

They'll go on arguing about who invented the movies for decades to come and the big dollar brigade keep insisting that the American Thomas Edison was the Father of the Cinema.

They tried that during the lifetime of inventive Bristol photographer William Friese-Greene who promptly went to the U.S. courts to point out that he had patented his invention before Edison. He won.

William was born in 1855 and lived behind where today's Council House now stands on College Green. He became a photographer and did very well, expanding his business from a studio in Queen's Road to further studios in Bath and Plymouth.

He loved invention and patented schemes ranging from airship bombs and stereo colour film to X-ray apparatus.

Bristol was too small a world for this ambitious man and he moved to London in his early 30s. One project fascinated him – the possibility of moving film, one which dated back to a moment he saw shadows created by passers-by reflected through blinds. How could he capture those fleeting images? At last he found the solution.

On June 21st, 1889 he took out Patent No. 10131 for a projector which took and showed moving pictures by using opaque film with slotted holes which could be run through a camera to record scenes in close sequence. The soon-to-be-familiar movie camera, no less.

Any more proof needed? William even sent Edison precise details of the mechanism involved because he hoped to interest the American in a joint project to ally Edison's phonograph with the Friese-Greene camera.

And Edison, so-called Father of Cinema, never replied.

Eddie's fatal last step

Eddie Cochran, top American rock'n'roller, took a last-minute decision that cost him his life one fatal night in Bristol.

Eddie had been appearing all week at the Bristol Hippodrome, heading a rock'n'roll variety package which also included fellow American Gene Vincent and youthful British rockers Billy Fury, Georgie Fame and Joe Brown.

The singer/songwriter who had scored worldwide hits with now-classic songs like 'C'mon Everybody', 'Somethin' Else' and 'Three Steps To Heaven' couldn't wait to get back to the States after his ten-week British tour.

On the day of the final show, Saturday April 16th 1960, he and Gene Vincent decided not to catch the late night train from Temple Meads to Paddington but to hire a cab to Heathrow instead. It would save time and all the hassle of travelling on to London Airport, they agreed.

Eddie, Gene, Eddie's girl-friend, songwriter Sharon Sheeley and a friend were collected by a Bristol taxi for the long journey up the Great West Road. They never reached their destination.

A tyre burst at Rowden Hill on the outskirts of Chippenham, the car swerved and it struck a lamp post. Eddie died in St Martin's Hospital, Bath, without recovering consciousness.

The distraught Sharon Sheeley was detained with back and leg injuries and comforted by the Everly brothers Don and Phil who raced to her bedside when they heard news of the tragedy as they arrived for their show in Bristol.

Cochran's records sell to this day . . . and each year a group of loyal fans hold a silent ceremony and lay a wreath by the roadside at Rowden Hill to mark his death.

*Rock'n'roll legend Eddie Cochran . . . his Bristol Hippodrome show was,
tragically, to prove his last.*

A Princely legacy

When the glamorous Prince of Wales, later to become King Edward VIII, visited Bristol on November 26th, 1934, one of his ports of call was to inspect a brand new, model council house in Lurgan Walk, Knowle West.

He met tenant William Bailey, an out-of-work labourer with eight children, and Mrs Bailey, who told the Prince of their delight with their new home after years in city centre slums.

So it's fitting that one of the very few monuments to a caring prince who spent his Royal visit to Bristol meeting the poor and the out-of-work can still be found not too far from Lurgan Walk.

It is in Hazelbury Road on the other side of the Wells Road in West Town, and it's one of the rare remaining pillar boxes erected during his brief reign.

Edward became King on January 20th, 1936, barely a year after his hugely successful visit to the poorer parts of Bristol. On December 11th he had abdicated so that he could marry Mrs Simpson, the woman he loved.

And all he left in Bristol were a few pillar boxes and some memories of the day the world's then most famous prince met the poor of Bristol.

Weather clock-watching

Take a look at the massive tidal rise and fall of the waters of the River Avon between the old Bristol City Docks and Avonmouth and you'll realise how crucial the winds were in the days of sailing ships.

A fair-ish breeze in the right direction could make all the difference between the safe arrival or departure of a vessel along that tricky river route, or disaster on the mudbanks.

So when the Commercial Rooms were opened as the Commercial Coffee House in Corn Street in 1811, one piece of information its shipping business members needed to know was the direction of the prevailing wind.

The club obliged . . . by providing a clock with a weather vane face overlooking the main Great Room. Those with ships to sail kept a close weather eye for any changes – and dashed off to give their orders if the wind swung into a favourable direction.

The clock is still there, the weather vane too. But today high-rise offices disguise true wind direction and, anyway, there are no ships to rush in or out of the City Docks should the weather change.

Left: *Edward VIII was never crowned but he was on the throne long enough to be celebrated by this post-box in West Town, Bristol.* Below: *the weather-watcher's guide to those vital winds . . . the weather 'clock' at the Commercial Rooms.*

The wonderful Horse Bazaar

It was planned as a gracious covered entry for the smartest carriages, became Bristol's best-known auction hall for horses . . . and was almost lost after years as a grubby car park.

That is the colourful story of the dramatic natural amphitheatre which lies through an archway beside Brunel House on St George's Road behind the Council House.

Once this imposing building was the Royal Western Hotel, a stopping-off place for transatlantic travellers about to board the steamship the *Great Western.*

And through the archway on the Park Street side of the hotel was the Bazaar Ride, where coaches and carriages could arrive beneath a large covered area and passengers disembark in comfort in all weathers.

When the transatlantic trade vanished, the large area with its cliff background became the Horse Bazaar, Bristol's best-known horse-dealing centre in the final days before the tram, bus and car dominated transport.

The old Horse Bazaar languished as a car park for many years and, like its illustrious hotel neighbour, was threatened with clearance and redevelopment. But the mood changed, restoration and heritage became the names of the game and both have been restored.

Today the old Horse Bazaar is attractively landscaped and a delight to the Bristol City Council staff who work in the redeveloped Brunel House, the modern offices built behind the original façade.

28

Bristol's corner of a foreign field

The Continent has countless 'corners of a foreign field' where British troops fell and lie buried and which are places of pilgrimage for their friends, relatives and descendants.

But Bristol has its own tiny corner which serves the same purpose for two German families and their friends.

They are the relatives and former comrades of the 26-year-old Hans Tiepelt and the 20-year-old Herbert Brosig, two German airmen who were buried with full Military Honours at Greenbank Cemetery in Bristol.

Tiepelt was pilot and Brosig wireless operator aboard a long range Messerschmitt Bf 110 long-range fighter which took part in the unsuccessful raid on the Parnall aircraft factory at Yate on September 27th, 1940, two days after the daring and devastating attack on the Bristol Aeroplane Company's works at Filton.

The two young German airmen must have been hoping for another success over Bristol's skies – but this time the RAF was ready and their fighter was pounced on by a Hurricane high over Fishponds.

The Luftwaffe plane was hit and fell with a chilling howl that reached screaming point as it disintegrated and smashed into a roof and courtyard at Stapleton Institution, now Manor Park Hospital, in a mass of blazing petrol.

The remains of the two men were gathered and now lie in peace in their Bristol graveyard.

A.E.J. Collins, the little lad with the biggest hitting record in cricket's history.

A.E.J. Collins' historic innings

Check the Guinness Book of Records and it's still there . . . highest individual cricketing score, A.E.J. Collins, 1899.

He was Arthur Edward James Collins, born in India in 1885 and a judge's son. He had lost both parents by the time he came to Bristol to board at Clark's House, the Victorian villa on the corner of Guthrie and Northcote roads.

He was a popular, sporty boy who, on Thursday June 22nd, 1899, aged 13, was captain of the Clark's XI in a match against the Junior XI of North Town house. He won the toss, put in his side to bat and opened the batting himself.

The game was played on an outfield off Guthrie Road with a poor surface and limited boundaries on all but one side. So on the long boundary, all hits had to be run and the short boundaries only counted for two.

Collins hit his first stroke at 3.30 p.m. and, by close of play at 6 p.m., he had scored 200.

On Friday lessons allowed another two-and-a-half hours' play and by then news of an exceptional innings had gone round the school.

'So brilliant was his play that even the Old Cliftonian match lost all its interest and quite a large crowd watched the boy's phenomenal performance.'

Young Arthur's innings almost ended at 400 when an easy catch was dropped but he went on to equal the existing highest scoring record of 485 and finished that day's play with 509.

The match resumed on Monday June 26th, with just 55 minutes to play after lessons. Collins reached 598 but he was running out of partners.

And on Tuesday June 27th, 1899, after just 25 minutes' play, Arthur lost his final partner with his personal score on 628. He had played less than seven hours' cricket with limited boundaries.

Collins went on to become a good sporting all-rounder, he joined the army and he hated being reminded of his schoolboy feat.

Lieutenant Collins of the Royal Engineers survived only a handful of weeks in France before dying in the opening battles of World War I.

The true ghostly Sarah

It's long been claimed that the lady in black who haunts the beautiful old Theatre Royal in King Street, home of the Bristol Old Vic, is none other than the great actress Sarah Siddons.

There are similar tales of Siddons' hauntings at other theatres but why should she haunt the Theatre Royal where she rarely appeared and where nothing momentous happened to her?

The answer is that the Theatre Royal's dark lady is indeed the ghost of a Sarah, but not Sarah Siddons. She is the wraith of Sarah, mistress and then wife and widow of actor/manager William Macready. He ran the theatre in Victorian times and after his death his widow kept the place going through very difficult times, sometimes paying actors' wages from her own pocket when box office takings were poor.

She is never seen in parts of the theatre built after her day and she is not unpleasant. At her worst she can be annoying and silly, making lights spin or appearing in the auditorium as she keeps an eye on the theatre she helped save from bankruptcy.

'Seeing Sarah' has become a Theatre Royal tradition, but over the years her name became muddled with that of another, more famous Sarah.

But Sarah isn't the only spook at the Theatre Royal . . .

The Old Vic's other ghost

He's called Richard, he worked in the paint shop making and painting scenery, he died in a tragic accident and stage staff come across him from time to time.

He was working on the mighty frame, a huge easel used for painting big backdrops, raised and lowered by a very large wheel. A cog failed to engage, the frame plummeted and the flying handle of the wheel smashed into his head, killing him.

The actor Nigel Stock, famous for his stage, TV and film appearances, once entered the paint shop and froze at a particular spot . . . Richard's spot. He told the painters he knew the place was haunted.

He wasn't telling them anything new. They were well used to the ghost which stands just out of direct eyesight but which moves objects and even sends some shooting across the room.

The paint shop staff have got used to Richard and his occasional visits . . . but they wish that instead of playing tricks on them he'd get to work and paint some of the scenery at night.

Not one but two ghosts haunt the Theatre Royal premises of the Old Vic company in King Street.

33

How Bristol beat Columbus

In 1492, the story goes, Christopher Columbus discovered the New World.

Wrong, very wrong.

In the first place, millions of American natives knew all about their homeland. Secondly, Norse sailors had built a short-lived settlement in Newfoundland centuries before Columbus.

And thirdly, at least a decade before Columbus, Bristol sailors had discovered the cod-rich seas off Newfoundland and landed to split, salt and dry their catches for transport back to Europe, particularly to Spain and Portugal.

The evidence can be found in a court case which took place while Columbus was still dreaming of a transatlantic trade route.

In 1481 Bristol customs officer Thomas Croft was charged with contributing towards the cost of a voyage by a Bristol ship which had sailed west with 40 bushels of salt. Customs officers were not allowed to trade.

Croft pleaded it had been a voyage of exploration to find and examine 'a certain Isle of Brasil', not a trading mission, and he was cleared.

The salt, in fact, had been used to cure the fish Bristol sailors had found on a previous trading voyage after being banned from the cod-rich waters of Iceland a little earlier.

Tongues wag in taverns and those of Bristol sailors may have been a little too well-oiled by wine when selling their dried cod in Spain. Columbus seems to have learned of Bristol's fishy secret.

A secret letter from an English spy to the so-called discoverer of the New World pretty well clinches the matter. It reads, 'It is considered certain that the cape of the said land was discovered in the past by men from Bristol . . . as your Lordship well knows'.

Right: The statue of Cabot gazes west from the City Docks . . . but men of Bristol almost certainly beat not only Cabot but Columbus too in the race for the New World.

Sweet-toothed success

In 1992 the British press hailed the 60th anniversary of the Mars bar as if it were an event worth fussing about . . . and no wonder Bristol's sweet-makers looked scornful.

Sixty years old? Pah! A mere nothing to a sweet-toothed city which was in at the very start of the chocolate business back in the mid-eighteenth century and whose entrepreneurial founding father of the sweet shop announced in 1756:

'The best sorts of chocolate, made and sold wholesale and retail by Joseph Fry, Apothecary, in Small Street, Bristol'.

Fry's grew and grew, opening new factories in what is now the Broadmead area of Bristol while increasing the range of products. By the 1920s central Bristol had become too congested for this ever-growing industry so, in 1921, the company moved to its green field site at Somerdale, Keynsham.

Many of Fry's famous brand names have lasted and lasted . . . but none has done as well as Fry's Chocolate Creams, first introduced in 1853. Chocolate Creams were born when Queen Victoria was in her early 30s and they're still going strong.

Mars at 60? Hmm . . . a mere stripling by Bristol standards.

The door to nowhere

It's a puzzle that fascinates pedestrians and motorists as they walk or drive down past the steep corner from Granby Hill into Hope Chapel Hill . . . a smart, very attractive period doorway which hangs in mid air.

There's a big drop below and not a stair to be seen to allow visitors to cross the threshold without risking their necks.

The house is Rutland House, a handsome Georgian building and the reason for that peculiar entrance can be dated back to the 1970s when the house was converted into flats.

All went well until the designers realised that the front door wasn't of any practical use to the new design – but that the door was protected as an historic feature of Clifton.

The door . . . but not, oddly enough, the stairs leading to the door. They weren't listed as of any interest at all.

So the door was sealed up, the stairs removed and the conversion completed, leaving Hope Chapel Hill with one of Bristol's most bizarre domestic entrances.

Watch that door, it leads to nowhere. The curious doorway in Hope Chapel Hill.

The Clifton Arcade, open at last after generations as a lock-up depository.

Clifton's shopping Cinderella

For more than a century it lay forgotten and unloved, the fanciful covered shopping centre that Joseph King designed to be the smartest shopping mall in the West Country.

The Royal Bazaar and Winter Gardens would attract the rich and the famous who would be enchanted by the two storeys of shop-fronts within this charming little shopping mall on Boyce's Avenue, between Victoria Square and busy Regent Street.

It never even opened. Just as the lovely arcade was completed in 1878, architect Mr King ran out of money and, not long afterwards, the open spaces and shops which should have been a busy scene of commerce and chatter became a silent furniture storehouse and depository.

Generations of shopkeepers who traded in the adjoining premises peered into this neglected Victorian wonderland with amazement and, from time to time, there were efforts to realise Mr King's dream.

By the 1980s the frontage had become so dangerous that it was shored up with ugly scaffolding, further scarring Mr King's creation.

But now at last, more than 110 years after the galleries and shops were completed, the Royal Bazaar and Winter Gardens has come to life at last.

The arcade is open and there are, at the time of writing, ambitious plans to turn it into that shoppers' paradise that Mr King dreamt of all those years ago.

NSM – No Thanks!

It was the loudest 'No' in Bristol's smoky history after tobacco giants Wills announced the biggest revolution in smoking since Sir Walter Raleigh introduced tobacco from the New World to the Court of Queen Elizabeth.

By the 1970s the anti-smoking health campaign had reached such proportions that Wills and other cigarette giants decided that if you couldn't beat 'em, you could try to woo 'em.

And Wills did so with NSM or New Smoking Material. The idea was cunningly simple. Cut down on tobacco, give cigarette smokers a substitute to puff on and, hey presto, smoking could be acceptable as a healthy pursuit once more. In June, 1977 the new-style cigarettes were launched in a fanfare of publicity.

It didn't work. In fact it failed so catastrophically that within three months of the much-advertised launch of safer ciggies, Wills' directors realised they had a huge turkey on their hands.

What to do with all those unwanted packets of fags? Set fire to them in the biggest bonfire in Bristol's tobacco history when more than 100 million NSM 'gaspers' were cremated.

Wills claimed foul, accusing the government of torpedoing their new products by not allowing a price advantage over the more tar-filled standards cigs. The public didn't agree. NSM lacked the nicotine kick that smokers crave . . . it was as simple as that.

When Buffalo Bill came to town

It was the biggest superstar show Bristol had ever seen . . . 12 performances over six days by the then top name in thrilling spectacle, Buffalo Bill and his Wild West Pioneer Exhibition.

Colonel William Cody, to give him his real name, brought four train loads of Red Indians, cowboys, buffaloes, horses, ponies, stage coaches and extras . . . so many that when they processed up the Gloucester Road on their way from Temple Meads station to their show site on Horfield Common on Sunday September 26th, 1891, onlookers reckoned the parade was a mile long.

Today Cowboys and Indians are old hat. But when Buffalo Bill made his triumphant visit to Bristol, the fictional Wild West was considered the most romantic, colourful place in the world and Colonel Cody its most famous character.

A 15,000 seat stadium was built on Horfield Common for the twice-daily performances which included spectacles like Buffalo Bill's single combat with Yellow Hand, an attack on a train by Red Indians and daredevil riding and shooting displays.

The ticket sellers proclaimed that 'Colonel W.F. Cody Will Positively Appear At Every Performance' and the punters poured in, more than 100,000 of them paying a shilling a ticket to watch the show of a lifetime.

The self-publicising giant of the Wild West world watched his train-loads of riders and animals return to Temple Meads at the end of the week and drawled 'I'm well satisfied.'

Right: *Howdy, pardners! Buffalo Bill caused a sensation when he brought his circus to town.*

Those headphones, that look of the serene Walkman wearer . . . the gargoyle at Wills Hall of Residence, Stoke Bishop.

The three kings gaze out from their niches at Fosters almshouses in Colston Street.

Bristol's first Walkman wearer?

Headphone-wearing youngsters walking Bristol's streets with their personal stereos playing away have been a familiar sight for some years now . . . but a student with a Walkman when grandad was still in his teens? Impossible, you might say.

But you'd be wrong. There he is, as clear as day, the zapped-out character with the headphones, the long hair and the beatific grin of someone listening to the latest sounds at full volume.

'He' is made of stone and he is one of the many grotesques designed by the artist Jean Hahn who was commissioned by the distinguished architect Sir George Oatley to provide the decorations for the lavish Wills Hall of Residence in Stoke Bishop. Hahn designed another set of heads for the Wills Memorial Building in Queen's Road, Clifton.

This gargoyle, thought to represent a physicist or electrical engineer, looks so modern that it's hard to believe that it was carved by one of a group of local stonemasons in the 1920s.

As for those early headphones he's wearing, they were either meant for receiving the primitive wireless transmissions of the day or for use in a scientific or medical equipment experiment.

We three kings . . .

There they stand, surveying the traffic and the bustle of Colston Street . . . the Three Kings of Cologne.

The trio, sculpted by Bristol artist Ernest Pascoe, took up their places on their public niches in 1967 when the early sixteenth century Chapel Of The Three Kings of Cologne was re-opened and re-dedicated after extensive restoration.

The Three Kings? Yes, of course, they are the Three Wise Men of the Nativity, Balthazar, Caspar and Melchior and their name was chosen by Bristol merchant John Foster when he added the chapel in 1504 to the adjoining almshouses he had founded 20 years before.

It is said that John Foster decided to honour the famous three after a visit to Cologne where he was particularly struck by the shrine honouring the relics of the Three Wise Men, relics which had been moved to Germany from Milan and, before that, Constantinople.

The 1967 renovation of the chapel also included the creation of a new stained glass window showing the Three Kings greeting the infant Christ and Mary.

Broadmead . . . Bristol's inside-out shopping centre

When Bristol started rebuilding in the 1950s, it promised itself a shopping centre fitting for the Young Elizabeth age of the new Queen Elizabeth II.

The old, much-loved Wine Street/Castle Street shops had gone up in flames in the first big blitz of November 1940. The new centre, it was decided, would look towards the future.

Fine plans were prepared, creating four roomy, open piazzas on the square-shaped Broadmead area. Cars would be banned and the shops serviced in off-peak hours by lanes behind the piazzas. Pedestrians would rule.

It wasn't to be. Traders were horrified at the thought of a centre where motorists wouldn't be allowed to park outside their front door and jeered at the idea of traffic-free pedestrian precincts.

The traders won. The service lanes were widened into main roads with high street frontages, the piazzas shrank to grubby service areas behind the shops and Broadmead was blighted.

But those original designers had the last laugh. Today the roads the traders demanded have become pedestrian precincts and Broadmead's biggest attraction is the car-free Galleries shopping mall.

You can still see those shrunken piazzas, an unsightly monument to a short-sighted past.

The Clifton slide

There it is, a marble-like track of limestone rubbed smooth by generations of children's trousers and skirts on the helter-skelter ride down the diagonal raft of rock just below the Observatory in Clifton.

No one can remember when children began turning a narrow lane of the rock surface into a shiny chute . . . but then no one can remember when children didn't shriek and squeal and risk their necks on this rough-and-tumble ride down to the zig-zag path below.

The authorities try to fence it off, but no restrictions in the world would stop daredevils 'bottoming' it down just as their great-great-grandparents did.

In Italian art circles, the Clifton slide has a far loftier reputation. Shortly after winning Britain's top art award, the Turner Prize in 1990, the Bristol-based artist Richard Long who creates landscape works like stone circles and gravel lanes in remote parts of the world was interviewed by a leading Italian art critic.

Long told of how the Clifton Downs had been an inspiration in his early days and he took the Italian writer for a walk up on the Downs. As they passed the bottom of the slide he pointed out the dramatic sight and joked 'My first serious piece of sculpture'.

The Italian critic took the gag seriously, and it was duly reported.

Cabot's whalebone gift

Of all Bristol's offbeat relics, the gigantic hoop of bone slung so carefully with its base resting on a cherubic head in St Mary Redcliffe Church must be the most bizarre and wonderful.

It is the rib of a cow whale and it came to Bristol, so the legend goes, as one of the only mementoes of the historic journey made by the Genoese-born adventurer John Cabot when he crossed the Atlantic in 1497.

Cabot had made an unsuccessful attempt to cross the Atlantic the year before. But it was in 1497, aboard the Bristol-made ship the *Matthew* with a crew of just 18 he reached Newfoundland.

And there, or on one of his brief landings as he explored the eastern coast of America, he presumably found the great length of bone so carefully preserved in Bristol's fairest parish church.

There was another yarn told about the bone . . . that it was a rib from a gigantic cow killed by Guy, Earl of Warwick. This story stems from the fact that there is a similar whale bone preserved in Warwick Castle.

Sceptics doubt that Cabot brought the bone back aboard the *Matthew*. Enthusiasts are sure that it was his gift to Bristol. Either way, it's a curiosity not to be missed.

Bristol's forgotten war memorial

A hundred people will pass St Andrew's Church for every one who pauses, surprised by the long, wide, slightly raised terrace at the Clifton Hill end of what is sometimes called Birdcage Walk.

The walk is a lovely avenue of pleached lime trees between Queen's Road and Clifton Hill, passing through a churchyard. But where is the church?

It was St Andrew's Church and its churchyard has a fascinating collection of tombs and memorials, but St Andrew's itself died on the first night of the Bristol Blitz, on Sunday November 24th, 1940.

The body of the church which had been built in the twelfth century, extended in the seventeenth century and replaced by a Regency Gothic church in the 1820s, was wrecked that night but the tower survived until 1958, when it was demolished.

The rubble was razed and removed, the ground cleared but the bones of the church's outline left in the earth as a reminder of those dreadful nights. A plaque explains the story to those rare few who do stop to examine this extraordinary war memorial.

A plaque and the stone outline of St Andrews, the church which died in the first Bristol blitz on Sunday November 24th, 1940.

The posh pawnshop's discreet entrance

It wasn't just the poor and working class who used Bristol's many pawnshops in the bad old days, 'quality' folk weren't above the services of the pawnbroker when times were hard.

The smartest – and those with the most to lose should they be spotted by their respectable friends and neighbours and even, in some cases, wives and husbands – used the oh-so-discreet services of Messrs Chillcotts in Park Street.

Park Street was and is a very, very public place and one of the West Country's most famous shopping streets, so no self-respecting person would be seen dead trying to pawn a bit of the family silver in the main shop.

So instead Chillcotts installed a hatch at the back of the shop which shy pawners could use at night. Goods to be pawned could be slipped through the hatch with the owner's name attached. Goods went down a chute to the back room and owners claimed the ticket the following day – using the back door in Great George Street for added discretion – when staff could make a discreet offer without causing embarrassment.

Bristol's best for Good Queen Bess

Bristol put out all the flags, painted its public monuments and provided nothing but the best when Queen Elizabeth I arrived in Bristol on August 14th, 1574 at the start of a week-long visit.

And there is one reminder of her visit in which Bristol staged mock battles, fired several salutes and laid on sumptuous feasts for Her Majesty and her court.

It is the superb saddle cloth the Queen used when she rode into Bristol on a white horse and it is now lovingly preserved by the Society of Merchant Venturers at Merchants' Hall in Clifton.

The blue velvet cloth is decorated with wonderful silver ornaments and solid silver stirrups, a marvellous reminder of an extraordinary visit.

The Queen stayed at the Great House on St Augustine's Back, on the site of what is now the Colston Hall and the cloth she had sat on was carefully put aside and presented by Bristol Corporation to Thomas Colston, the High Sheriff of the county. It stayed in the family until the family seat at Roundway, Devizes was sold in 1947.

The cloth was one of many lots which came up for sale and it was snapped up by Sir Foster Robinson who brought it back to Bristol and presented it to the Merchants.

The Grey Friars and the Black Death

Today the solitary reminder of the brave Grey Friars who nursed Bristol through its worst calamity is a fancy logo on an ugly office building. It is a poor memorial to men who sacrificed themselves for Bristol.

The Greyfriars building on Lewin's Mead stands on the site of an ancient friary which was the home of monks who did all they could when the Black Death brought its ghastly toll to Bristol in 1348.

The self-sufficient Friars had a friary surrounded by a small holding of orchards, vegetable gardens and other food-producing areas outside the city wall in their quiet community stretching from Lewin's Mead to the Kingsdown slopes.

When the Black Death struck, they saw their clear mission to help the 10,000 folk of Bristol.

This plague, so called because of the dark splotches it caused on the skin of its victims, created havoc in Bristol, the first British city to be overwhelmed by a fatal illness which cut a scythe through Asia and Europe.

Almost half the entire population of the crowded, insanitary little city that was olden-day Bristol died in the plague but the good Friars ignored all dangers to tend victims and give them a Christian burial.

The churchyards could not cope with the thousands of bodies so plague burial grounds were dug. One, by Temple Church, off Victoria Street, covered half an acre.

The dark tale behind Bristol's prettiest ceremony

Each year they troop down to the ancient crypt of St Nicholas Church, boarders at Bristol's oldest girls' school in their charming bonnets and capes and carrying lighted tapers.

They are pupils from Red Maids School in Westbury-on-Trym enacting an annual ceremony which dates back hundreds of years . . . and which recalls the days when Bristol was at its most violent.

The ceremony is the highlight of Founder's Day in honour of the merchant John Whitson, Mayor and Member of Parliament for Bristol and the man who left money in his will for a school for 40 local orphan girls who 'should go and be apparelled in red cloth' and be taught to read and sew.

But the ceremony doesn't commemorate any conventional anniversary like Whitson's death or the founding of the school. It marks his attempted murder on November 7th, 1626.

Whitson, as a Bristol worthy, was called in to settle a dispute between two people and one of them, Christopher Callowhill, became so enraged that he rushed at Whitson and stabbed him in the face with a dagger.

Whitson survived this terrifying attack and lived another two years before dying after a fall from a horse.

And it is the murder attempt, not his death, that the girls of Red Maids give thank for each year as they hold their beautiful candlelit service in costume each November.

The pub with the most rules

The Coronation Tap in Clifton is famous throughout the land as Britain's premier cider house.

Back in the 1960s it was as well known for its list of rules as it was for its cider. And that was all down to Mine Host with the Most Rules in Bristol.

The late 'Dick' Bradstock ruled the Tap with a rod of iron, insisting that cider's poor image as a troublemakers' tipple could be improved in a well-disciplined house. And discipline is what he imposed with his Six Nos.

NO use of the word 'Scrumpy'. Any would-be drinker demanding scrumpy would be instantly shown the door. The correct request was for 'dry' or 'rough', 'medium' or 'sweet', depending on your taste.

NO large drinks for women. The request for a pint for a woman meant a walk . . . to another pub. Strictly halves for ladies.

NO moving furniture. If a stool was moved from an empty table to a crowded one, Mr Bradstock shot out from behind the bar to bellow 'OUT!'

NO signs of affection. Even married couples took care to ensure that they did not so much as hold each other's hands in Mr Bradstock's sight.

NO spirits. Ask for a whisky and soda and you risked the wrath of the landlord. Cider and beer only!

NO scruffy hair/clothes. When wearing mock uniforms à la Sgt Pepper came into style, it most definitely was NOT a fashion Mr Bradstock approved.

But he held few grudges, allowed prodigals to return after their misdemeanours and the Coronation Tap flourished . . . despite those NOs.

The Penn Memorial at St Mary Redcliffe Church . . . William Penn invented the American garden.

America the beautiful . . . thanks to William Penn

The bad news of Bristol's links with the New World are well known. Slavery, exploitation and greed are by-words for the trade Bristol skilfully exploited in the heyday of early colonialism.

The good news gets less of a show – particularly how Bristol's William Penn invented the American garden.

Today English and European gardens rule the roost, but there's a rapidly growing interest in America's classic gardens . . . and for that you can thank the tree and flower-loving Mr Penn.

William was son of Admiral Sir William Penn, a leading figure in the Civil War who helped restore Charles II to the throne. William, by contrast, was a peaceful creature and when his father died, the King, who owed the Penns a fortune, traded land for cash . . . 47,000 acres of American land. William and his Quaker community sailed over to America to make their own new colony, Pennsylvania.

William was so keen on gardens that on founding Pennsylvania in 1682 he declared, 'Let every house be placed in the middle of its plot so there may be ground on each side for gardens or orchards or fields.'

It was a revolutionary idea from a man brought up in overcrowded Bristol . . . and he didn't stop there.

A few years later came the edict, 'Every owner of a house should plant one or more trees before the door that the town may be well shaded from the violence of the sun.'

The garden city had arrived . . . thanks to a Bristolian.

Bristol's Rolling Stones

Mick and Keith, Brian and Bill and, of course, Charlie were already world-famous as the Rolling Stones, pop music's favourite rebels, by the autumn of 1965.

They'd just celebrated their biggest hit of all, '(I Can't Get No) Satisfaction' when word came through that a Bristol band were claiming that they, not Jagger, Richards, Jones, Wyman and Watts, were the original Rolling Stones.

And it was all too true. Bristol's Rolling Stones were the three Stone brothers who'd formed their own skiffle band at the height of the Lonnie Donegan era and played gigs like the Bristol Press Ball in 1957.

Skiffle came from American blues music which often featured light travelling heroes described as rolling stones, so it was a good title.

The washboard group had changed their name to the Stone Brothers to avoid confusion when Mick, Keith and co. sprang to fame after taking their name from bluesman Muddy Waters' classic 'Rolling Stone', but the matter still rankled.

'We have no desire for the Jagger Stones to change their name. We only want to establish that the Bristol Stones are entitled to the name and were the first Rolling Stones,' the group announced.

Top rock promoter/agent Tito Burns, then representing Mick, Keith and the rest chortled, 'This would make a wonderful film.'

The Bristol Stones even consulted lawyers, but the matter ended quietly and amicably . . . and almost no one remembers the original Rolling Stones.

The trickiest five miles of all

It's just five miles from Bristol City Docks to the Severn at Avonmouth but there wasn't a sea captain of old who didn't fear that journey.

The twisting route to the estuary has one of the highest tides in the world. The brimful, beautiful Avon in its gorge setting rapidly becomes an ominous ships' graveyard when the waters fall to reveal the mud-banked dangers below.

The most famous of the Avon's countless victims was the *Demerera*, built in Bristol as a paddle steamer in 1851 and then only second to the S.S. *Great Britain* as the world's largest ship.

She was launched on September 27th and was towed by tug from the City Docks on November 10th to have her engines fitted in Glasgow. The tide was ebbing fast and she had barely passed the then unfinished Clifton Suspension Bridge when she became well and truly stuck in the mud.

The great ship blocked the busy entrance to Bristol docks as she swung across the river and huge crowds gathered to watch the frantic operation to get her safely afloat and so re-open the port.

They got her off in the end, but the *Demerera* was declared a loss by her underwriters. But the creator of Bristol's biggest marine traffic jam won her place in history – she was re-fitted with sails, was re-named the *British Empire* and so became the world's largest sailing vessel.

One that didn't make it . . . the good ship 'Refuge' stranded on Leigh Bank in 1854. The huge rise and fall of the Avon stranded many ships over the centuries.

*The Clifton Rocks Railway
then and now . . . once it
was one of Bristol's top
tourist attractions.*

56

Clifton Rocks Railway

There's an optimistic piece of graffiti on the rusty gates of the old Clifton Rocks Railway. It reads: Re-opening soon. Well, maybe, the cynics might say.

But here, hidden by the cliff faces of the Avon Gorge, is one of late Victorian England's most fascinating railways lines. . . and a fabulous tourist attraction in its day.

This 45 degree, four-car furnicular line was built to link Clifton with the important steamer, rail and tram connections below, on the site of the present Portway.

It opened on March 11th, 1893 and was an instant success. On the opening day 6,220 people went up and down the line and in the first year the passenger figures reached 437,492.

The railway was a huge tourist attraction and on Bank Holidays it regularly carried more than 1,000 an hour. Its busiest day of all came on July 5th, 1913 when the Royal Show was staged on the Downs. That day it carried 14,300 people.

There were lovely stations at each end to greet passengers as they rose or fell on a clever water balance system . . . the railcars' tanks were filled at the upper station with enough water to raise the opposite cars below. The tanks were emptied below and the water pumped up to the top station and so on. Neat, efficient and energy saving.

But the opening of the Portway in the 1920s and the disruption of the tram, steamer and rail connections killed off the line's trade and, in 1934, the railway was shut down. The vault of the tunnel remains virtually intact, a sleeping beauty of Victorian invention which could, perhaps, be revived. There have been attempts.

The fanciful Priory in Sion Hill, once the smallest private home open to the private in Britain.

The flamboyant Priory

Take that famous walk up towards the Clifton Suspension Bridge past the Avon Gorge Hotel and you can't fail to notice one of Bristol's most flamboyant homes, St Vincent Priory in Sion Hill.

With its soaring windows and extraordinary ornaments, it looks as if it must be the home of a larger-than-life character . . . and it certainly has been over the years.

The Gothic revival house was built in the early nineteenth century and legend has it that the site has some monastic background. One refers to a religious sanctuary in caves below today's building.

It was home to confidence trickster Tom Provis in the mid-nineteenth century. He had an unsuccessful claim to be the rightful heir to the great Ashton Court estate across the Avon and was transported to Australia for his pains.

In the 1960s the Priory was bought by colourful artist George Melhuish who, after letting the place to students for a few years, took over the place himself, opened it to the public and took great pride in announcing that his was the smallest private home open to the public in Britain.

When George Melhuish died in 1985, he left the five-storey house to the Bristol City Art Gallery with the proviso that it opened to the public to display his paintings and furniture. Bristol reluctantly turned down his offer and the Priory was sold.

From a castle to a street

Bristol Castle was one of the grandest, noblest Norman castles of them all. A magnificent building created by Robert of Gloucester in the 1120s when he extended the smaller, original castle on the banks of the Avon.

You'll see a few hummocks and bits of wall – even a stairway leading to a cellar – on what has now become Castle Park next to the Galleries shopping centre.

But most of the castle lies a little down the road . . . underneath Castle Street.

Because when Oliver Cromwell was tidying up England after the Civil War, he looked long and hard at Bristol Castle with its massive walls and defences and didn't like what he saw. It would be all too easy for trouble-makers to use this massive pile as a refuge. So in 1656 Cromwell gave the order – Demolish Bristol Castle.

The statues of Brennus and Belinus flanking St John's Gate.

Easy to say, rather harder to do. At first Bristol householders were ordered to do or pay for a day's work a week to bring the castle down but after several months the place looked as sturdy as ever.

So the Corporation hired labourers who dismantled one of Norman Britain's greatest masterpieces and then turned the stones to the best use they could think of.

That was to use the remains of Robert of Gloucester's castle as the foundations of a brand new road outside what had been the castle walls. You can see it today. It's called, fittingly, Castle Street.

Brennus, Bristol's legendary founder

Two seated statues flank lovely old St John's Gate, the gateway into walled Bristol which Queen Elizabeth I rode through on her visit to the city.

They were statues of legendary, far, far earlier rulers of this land, the brother-kings Brennus and Belinus, sons of King Malmutius and Queen Conwenna.

When the old king died, the kingdom was divided. Brennus inherited all the lands north of the Humber, Belinus everything to the south. Brennus was furious, declaring he'd been given a raw deal with his gift of all the roughest, most mountainous and least fertile lands while lucky Belinus had been awarded the best, richest parts of the kingdom.

The argument became so bitter that the brothers raised armies and were about to fight when their mother stepped in and separated the two sides. A deal was struck and the two decided to share all the lands.

Brennus is the legendary character the fables say founded Bristol, or The Place Of The Bridge. It's also said that the Romans later called the settlement at the junction of the Avon and the Frome – today's Bristol – Caer Bren or the City of Brennus.

Whatever the truth of the tale, there's one historical howler you can spot if you take a look at their Bristol statues. The brothers supposedly lived centuries before Christ . . . but both carry crucifixes.

William Watts' silver dream machine

It looks like a streamlined prison camp observation post and it's a poor replacement for one of Bristol's most fascinating industrial buildings.

'It' is the new Shot Tower in Cheese Lane, a drab monument to a time when Swinging Sixties just as often meant the swing of the demolition men's ball-and-chain as it did mini skirts and psychedelic pop.

November 1968 saw the Old Shot Tower demolished to make Redcliffe Hill a dual carriageway. So vanished Bristol's first brick-built building and the historic home of plumber William Watts who, in 1782, had a startling dream of molten lead being poured from a great height and falling into water in perfect little balls of lead shot.

He was so convinced that he dismantled his house, raised a tower and removed the kitchen floor flagstones so lead could fall freely from the roof into the deep well below and, amazingly, the trick worked! Molten lead trickled through his perforated frame, fell and formed into exactly the shapes he wanted.

What Watts didn't realise was that the lead he used, from the Mendips, contained arsenic, making his process possible. Without that added ingredient, the tumbling lead would not have formed tiny balls.

He was soon a rich man and sold the business to Sheldon Bush and Co. for £10,000, investing much of it in property speculation on the Clifton hillside. He came a cropper when developing Windsor Terrace on its cliff-like site and was almost bankrupted but he survived the tricky times of the Napoleonic Wars and was honoured by a gift of china by King George IV in 1820 to mark his achievement.

Right: *Watching . . . watching . . . the slightly sinister shot tower gazes out over Bristol.*

America . . . the continent named after a Bristolian?

Did America gets its name from the Bristol merchant who paid the lion's share of funding the successful transatlantic voyage by John Cabot in 1497?

Yes, say proud Bristolians, and it is certainly true that the man who did the most to raise the financial wind to speed Cabot and the *Matthew* west was one Richard Ameryk, merchant and collector of customs dues in the city.

The name Ameryk is Welsh – Ap Meuric, or Son of Maurice – and Richard lived just outside the city at Lower Court, Long Ashton. His married daughter Joan Brook has a memorial brass at St Mary Redcliffe Church.

Cabot, the story goes, raised the flags of England and St Mark when he made his historic landfall in the New World on Midsummer's Day, 1497 . . . and he named the land after his chief benefactor.

There is another school of thought, that the name America comes from one Amerigo Vespucci, another transatlantic voyager and a boastful character who claimed he had beaten Cabot to the mainland and so had the right to name the new land after himself.

A school of thought that patriotic Bristolians will dismiss as fanciful nonsense, of course.